Ronald Reagan

History Maker Bios

Jane Sutcliffe

BARNES & NOBLE

NEW YORK

For the staff of Tolland Public Library, with thanks

Text © 2008 by Jane Sutcliffe
Illustrations © 2008 by Lerner Publishing Group, Inc.

This 2008 edition published by Barnes & Noble, Inc.
by arrangement with Lerner Publications Company, a division of
Lerner Publishing Group, Inc., Minneapolis, MN.

Illustrations by Tad Butler

ISBN-13: 978-1-4351-0168-5
ISBN-10: 1-4351-0168-5

Printed and bound in the United States of America

1 3 5 7 9 10 8 6 4 2

TABLE OF CONTENTS

INTRODUCTION

Imagine being a movie star *and* president of the United States all in one lifetime. That's what Ronald Reagan did.

His smooth voice and good looks made him a popular actor. But it was his sharp wit that made him a successful politician. Reagan had a gift for making speeches. And people liked what he had to say. First, they elected him governor of California. Then they asked him to run for president. In time, Reagan became one of the most admired presidents ever to live in the White House.

This is his story.

DUTCH

Ronald Reagan was born on February 6, 1911, in Tampico, Illinois. But hardly anyone called him Ronald. To his friends and most of his family, he was Dutch. That's because his father said he looked like a "fat little Dutchman."

Dutch did most of his growing up in the town of Dixon, Illinois. He and his older brother, Neil, swam in the nearby Rock River in the summer. They went ice-skating in the winter.

Each summer for seven years, Dutch had a job as a lifeguard.

The Reagan house overlooked the high school football field. Dutch could hear the *whump* of the players' bodies as they tackled one another. He couldn't wait to wear the purple and white uniform of a Dixon High player.

Dutch got his chance. At Dixon High, he became an important player on the football team. By then, he had become a tall, handsome young man. He had dark hair and a sunny, bright smile. His eyesight was so poor that he wore thick glasses—except when he had his picture taken.

Dutch graduated from high school in 1928. In the fall he entered Eureka College, about one hundred miles from Dixon. A scholarship helped pay his way.

Eureka was a small school. Dutch would have been a hard person to miss. He was everywhere, doing everything. He played football, of course. But he was also a cheerleader for the basketball team and captain of the swim team. He had a job washing dishes and was a reporter for the school paper.

AND JUSTICE FOR ALL

Dutch's parents taught him to treat all people with respect. Skin color didn't matter. Neither did religion. Not everyone thought that way. Once, Dutch was traveling with his college football team. A hotel manager refused to give rooms to the black players on the team. So Dutch invited them to stay with his family nearby.

Dutch wasn't the best player on the Eureka football team, but he worked hard to get better.

He was a campus leader too. Once, the college planned to cut out some important classes. Many students were angry. Dutch was chosen to give a speech explaining the students' point of view. For the first time, he felt his words touch an audience.

Dutch had acted in school plays in high school. At college, he tried out for every play the drama club did. In his third year, Eureka was invited to take part in an acting competition. Dutch was named one of the six best actors in the contest. One professor told him he should think about making acting his career.

Dutch did think about it. He graduated from college in 1932. He needed a job. But being an actor seemed like too big a dream. He thought he might like to be a radio announcer, reporting on football games. He went from one radio station to another. Everyone said no.

Then he went to station WOC in Davenport, Iowa. The manager there decided to give him a chance. Before long, the voice of Dutch Reagan was a familiar one to area sports fans.

Shortly after getting the job at WOC, Dutch was transferred to an even bigger station, WHO.

Dutch, shown here in 1936, worked for WHO as a sports announcer.

Every spring, Dutch went to California to report on baseball spring training. Once, while he was there, he bumped into an old friend who had become an actress. He told her how much he wanted to be an actor. The friend offered to help.

She introduced Dutch to her agent. The agent liked Dutch. He set up a meeting at Warner Bros. Studios. Dutch had a screen test. He acted in a short scene from a movie. The screen test showed the studio how Dutch would look and sound in a movie.

When the test was over, Dutch was supposed to wait in California for the studio's decision. Instead, he went back to Iowa. He still had a job to do. But he couldn't help wondering if he was being a fool for leaving.

Two days later, Dutch got his answer. A message from the agent arrived. "WARNERS OFFERS CONTRACT . . . ," it read. "WHAT SHALL I DO?"

Dutch wasted no time sending his reply: "SIGN BEFORE THEY CHANGE THEIR MINDS."

At the age of twenty-six, he was going to Hollywood.

2 "THE GIPPER"

Dutch was a terrible name for an actor. At least, that's what the bosses at the movie studio decided. They had a meeting to come up with a better name.

"How about Ronald? . . . Ronald Reagan?" Dutch suggested.

"Hey, that's not bad," one of the bosses said. So Dutch became Ronald again.

Ronald's first movie was *Love Is on the Air*. He played a radio announcer. When that film was finished, he made another. And then another. In the next year and a half, he made eleven movies.

One of them was *Brother Rat*. His costar was a pretty young actress named Jane Wyman. Ronald and Jane made a handsome couple. Soon, newspapers were reporting that they were dating. On January 26, 1940, they were married.

Ronald and Jane Wyman were often photographed when they went out on dates.

Ronald usually waited for the studio to tell him which movie he should be in. But then he heard that Warner Brothers was going to make a football movie. And Ronald just *had* to be in that movie.

The movie was *Knute Rockne—All-American*. Ronald won the part of football star George Gipp. In one scene, Gipp asks his coach to have the players "Win just one for the Gipper." After that, Ronald had a new nickname—the Gipper.

Ronald played the Gipper in KNUTE ROCKNE — ALL-AMERICAN.

Ronald was becoming one of the most popular stars in Hollywood. Only handsome actor Errol Flynn got more fan mail. At home, he and Jane had a new baby daughter, Maureen.

Then, in 1941, the United States entered World War II (1939–1945). Ronald was called to serve in the U.S. Army Air Corps. His poor eyesight kept him out of battles though. Instead, he stayed in Hollywood. He made movies training soldiers to do things like spot enemy airplanes.

Ronald's poor eyesight kept him from being a pilot in World War II. He could only play the part of a flier in training films like the one pictured here.

When the war was over, Ronald was ready for his life to get back to normal. He and Jane adopted a baby boy, Michael. And he was ready to make more movies like *Knute Rockne*. But Hollywood seemed to have forgotten about Ronald Reagan. He had trouble finding good parts.

So he found other things to do. Ronald had always been a leader. In 1947, he became president of the Screen Actors Guild (SAG). This group worked to protect the rights of actors. Ronald helped to make sure actors got fair pay and fair treatment. He impressed many people with his good ideas.

TELL US MORE, RONALD

Ronald liked to talk. And he *really* liked to talk about politics. Some of his actor friends thought he talked a little too much. If he didn't stop making speeches, one said, "he'll end up in the White House."

Ronald was spending more and more time working with SAG. At the same time, Jane was becoming more successful as an actress. Soon it was clear that they had little in common. In 1949, they divorced.

Around the same time, Ronald played in a baseball game with other actors. He crashed into another player and broke his leg in six places. He was on crutches for months. And there weren't many movie parts for an actor on crutches. Ronald could feel his career slipping away.

What would he do if he couldn't be an actor?

3 A New Path

Ronald continued as SAG president. One day, he got a call from a friend. An actress named Nancy Davis needed his help. It seemed there were two actresses by that name, and people were mixing them up. Ronald took Nancy to dinner to straighten things out. He began to see more and more of her.

Before long Ronald knew that he was in love. In 1952, he and Nancy were married. Later that year their daughter Patricia was born. (A son, Ronald Prescott, joined the family later.)

Ronald was still making a few movies a year. None were hits. It was clear that Ronald's movie career was over. It was time to try something new. In the 1950s, "something new" meant television.

The Reagan family in 1960: Ronald, Ron, Nancy, and Patti

General Electric Theater was on Sunday nights at nine o'clock for eight years.

In the early days of TV, shows were paid for by big companies. The company usually had its name in the title of the show. Ronald became the host of *General Electric Theater*. He introduced a different story every week.

As part of the job, he visited General Electric factories around the country. He gave speeches—lots of speeches. Audiences loved his stirring style of speaking.

At first, he just talked about life in Hollywood. Then he began talking about politics. He also listened. The workers told him that government had gotten too big. They said that there were too many laws taking away too much of their freedom.

Ronald had always thought that government was the answer to people's problems. Now he felt that government *was* the problem. And that's what he began to say in his speeches. His audiences loved it.

Ronald (LEFT) talks to workers at a General Electric plant in Illinois in 1955.

Ronald and Nancy attend an event.

When *General Electric Theater* ended, Ronald worked on other shows and made another movie. But some people thought that he should run for office. Instead, he helped other politicians.

In 1964, Barry Goldwater was running for president. To help, Ronald taped a speech for TV. For half an hour he spoke about big government and high taxes. He spoke with passion. At times, he was funny. When it was over, there was no question. Ronald Reagan was not just an actor anymore. He was a political leader.

California was getting ready to choose a new governor. Some Republicans thought that Reagan should run for the office. Reagan told them they were crazy. He hoped they'd find someone better.

They didn't. In 1966, Reagan ran for governor. He won by nearly one million votes. For years, Ronald Reagan had talked about the problems in government. As Governor Reagan, he could do something about them. And people liked what he did. In 1970, he was reelected.

The Reagans wave to the crowd at a victory celebration after the 1966 election.

Reagan always kept a jar of jelly beans on his desk. And he didn't mind sharing.

People expected Reagan to run again four years later. But he said no. He and Nancy had bought a big ranch in the mountains. He was looking forward to long days of riding horses.

At first, that's what happened. Then people began to call and write from all over the country. They wanted Reagan to run for president.

President! Reagan thought a lot about the idea as he rode his horse. He remembered something he had said in one of his speeches. "A candidate doesn't make the decision whether to run for president," he had said. "The people make it for him."

The decision was made.

4 MR. PRESIDENT

Reagan was a member of the Republican Party. He hoped the party would choose him to be their candidate for president. Then he would run against the Democrats' choice, Jimmy Carter.

That didn't happen. The Republican Party chose President Gerald Ford instead. But in the general election, Ford lost. In 1977, Jimmy Carter became president.

And Reagan? He went home to his ranch. And he waited to see what would happen.

Reagan (RIGHT) and Nancy enjoyed riding horses at their ranch in California.

He didn't like what he saw. Prices were going up. People were out of work. Many families could not afford to buy what they needed.

In the Middle Eastern country of Iran, there was an uprising. Rioters captured more than sixty Americans there. They were being held, blindfolded and helpless.

Reagan saw that Americans were losing pride in their country. That made him angry. It was time to do something.

Reagan accepts the Republican nomination for president.

In 1980, Reagan ran for president. In speech after speech, he told people about his plan to change the government. The government had gotten too big, he said. It was taking too much money away from people in taxes.

Instead, he had a plan to cut taxes. People would be able to keep more of their money. The government wouldn't have to spend so much to help needy families, Reagan said. Instead, he wanted more money for the country's army and navy. A strong military would keep the country safe.

Other politicians laughed at Reagan's plan. They said it would never work. But the American people liked his ideas. On January 20, 1981, Ronald Reagan became the country's fortieth president. That day, there was another reason to celebrate. The Americans who had been held in Iran were released and heading home.

Reagan got right to work shrinking the government. He worked hard to get new laws passed.

At the age of sixty-nine, Reagan became the oldest U.S. president elected. BELOW: He was sworn in to office on January 20, 1981.

On March 30, 1981, Reagan gave a speech at a Washington, D.C., hotel. Outside, as he was leaving, he heard a *pop,pop,pop*. Gunshots! At once, the men guarding Reagan pushed him into the waiting car. Then they sped away.

Reagan was in terrible pain. At first, he thought that he had broken a rib. At the hospital, he learned a bullet had hit him. It had stopped less than an inch from his heart.

Reagan spent the next two weeks in the hospital. He was sad to learn that three others had been shot too. But the gunman had been quickly caught.

LAUGHING WITH REAGAN

Reagan loved to make people laugh—even when he was hurt. When Nancy saw him in the hospital, he told her, "Honey, I forgot to duck." He told his doctor, "I hope you're a Republican."

"Today, Mr. President, we're all Republicans," the doctor replied.

Four days after being shot, Reagan was able to walk down the hall with Nancy.

Reagan was eager to get back to work. And there was plenty of work to do. Reagan's tax cuts meant less money was coming into the government. He knew that meant that the government would have to spend less. Instead, it was still spending too much. In fact, it was spending a lot more than it was taking in.

In his first speech after being shot, Reagan (CENTER LEFT) talked to the U.S. Congress about the economy.

Many people wanted the government to spend less on the military. That would save money. But Reagan said no. He wanted the country to be safe, no matter what it cost.

Reagan believed that the greatest danger to the United States was the Soviet Union. The two countries were not on friendly terms.

The Soviet Union was made up of Russia and nearby countries. It was a Communist nation. That meant that the government ran all businesses. People there could not own property. In the Soviet Union, people did not choose their own leaders. And they could not come and go as they wished.

SANDRA DAY O'CONNOR

As president, Reagan had promised to appoint the first woman to the Supreme Court. He kept his promise when he chose Sandra Day O'Connor. He said she was "the right woman for the job." She was sworn in (right) by Chief Justice Warren Burger (left) on September 25, 1981.

Reagan saw the Soviet Union as a great threat to other countries. Its ideas were in danger of spreading around the world. He even called the country "the evil empire."

At the same time, Reagan knew it was important to get along with the Soviet Union's leaders. Both countries had huge numbers of weapons. A war would be a disaster. Reagan wrote to the Soviet leaders. He wanted to meet face-to-face. But the answer was always no.

In 1984, Reagan was reelected. At about the same time, the Soviet Union had a new leader too. Would the leaders of the two countries finally be able to meet? Or was the world headed for war?

5 CHANGING A WORLD

The new leader of the Soviet Union was Mikhail Gorbachev. He was young and smart. Reagan liked him from the moment the two shook hands.

Over the next couple of years, the leaders met and talked. They didn't agree on everything—or even most things. But they agreed that a war between their countries must never happen. And they agreed to keep talking.

Day Of Sadness

In January 1986, a tragedy turned Reagan's attention away from the Soviet Union. On that day, the space shuttle *Challenger* exploded in the sky. All seven people on board died.

Reagan spoke to the American people on television. He spoke of the crew's bravery. He called them pioneers. "We will never forget them," he said. His words helped heal the nation's sadness.

Of course, Reagan wanted the Soviet leader to give his people more freedoms. And he wasn't afraid to say so.

Once, he gave a speech in Berlin, West Germany. Berlin was an unusual city. The western half of it was free. The eastern half was controlled by the Soviet Union. People on the east were not allowed to go to the west— even to visit relatives. A wall ran smack through the city to separate the two parts.

The Berlin Wall made Reagan angry. Gorbachev was not in West Berlin listening to Reagan's speech that day. But Reagan was speaking to him just the same. "Mr. Gorbachev, tear down this wall!" he thundered. He knew the Soviet leader would get the message.

Reagan gives his famous speech with the Berlin Wall in the background. He was interrupted twenty-eight times with applause.

Reagan was determined to keep Communism from spreading. But his determination led to problems. Some of his assistants were caught supplying money and weapons to a group called the contras. The contras were fighting a Communist government in another country. But helping them in their war was against U.S. law.

There was worse news. The aides had gotten the money by selling weapons to Iran. That was the country that had captured U.S. citizens several years earlier. Iran was still a threat to the United States. So selling weapons to that country broke even more laws.

In 1987, Reagan (BOTTOM RIGHT) meets in the Oval Office with the group investigating the Iran-Contra affair.

In 1987, Reagan went on television to talk to the American people about Iran-Contra.

Reagan insisted that he hadn't known what his assistants had done. But, as president, he had been in charge. Their actions were his responsibility.

"Iran-Contra" was a mistake, he said. But when you make a mistake, "you take your knocks, you learn your lessons, and then you move on." He was ready to move on.

In December 1987, Ronald and Nancy Reagan welcomed some very important guests. Mr. and Mrs. Gorbachev came to visit. Bright red Soviet flags flew all around the White House in their honor.

The two leaders still agreed that their countries' weapons were a danger to the world. And this time, they did more than talk. They agreed to destroy thousands of nuclear weapons. No other countries had ever done that before. When they signed their names to the treaty, they made history.

Gorbachev (LEFT) and Reagan sign a treaty to take apart thousands of nuclear weapons.

A few months later, it was Reagan's turn to be the visitor. He and Nancy traveled to Moscow, in the Soviet Union. Reagan was thrilled to speak to cheering students at Moscow University. A reporter asked him if he still thought the country was the "evil empire." "No," Reagan said. "I was talking about another time in another era."

Reagan and Gorbachev talk in front of Saint Basil's Cathedral in Moscow in 1988.

By 1989, Reagan had spent eight years as president. His job was done. He had changed the way people thought about government. He had changed the way the United States and the Soviet Union thought about each other. In his last speech to the American people, he said, "We meant to change a nation, and instead, we changed a world. . . . All in all, not bad, not bad at all."

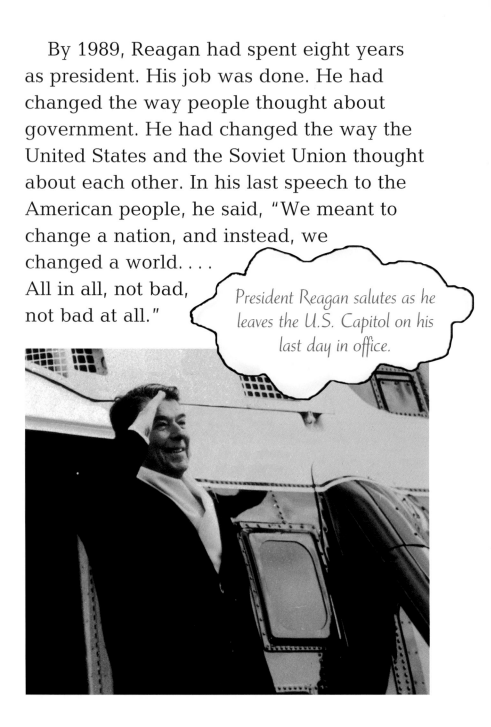

President Reagan salutes as he leaves the U.S. Capitol on his last day in office.

Reagan and Nancy went home to their ranch in California. In 1994, Reagan announced that he had Alzheimer's disease. The disease affected his brain. A lifetime of memories was being lost.

Ronald Reagan died on June 5, 2004. He was ninety-three. At his funeral, leaders from all over the world came to honor him. Among them was his old enemy and friend Mikhail Gorbachev. He called Reagan "an extraordinary political leader." And he called him "a peacemaker."

All in all, not bad, not bad at all.

TIMELINE

In the year . . .

1920 Reagan moved with his family to Dixon, Illinois.

1928 he graduated from Dixon High School.

1932 he graduated from Eureka College and became a radio sports announcer.

1937 he made his first movie. | Age 26

1940 he married Jane Wyman.

1941 his daughter Maureen was born in January. he began serving in the U.S. Army Air Corps in December.

1945 his son Michael was adopted.

1947 Reagan became president of the Screen Actors Guild.

1948 he and Jane were divorced.

1952 he married Nancy Davis in March. his daughter Patricia was born in October.

1954 he became host of *General Electric Theater*.

1958 his son Ronald Prescott was born.

1966 Reagan was elected governor of California. | Age 55

1980 he was elected president of the United States. | Age 69

1981 he was shot in front of a Washington, D.C., hotel.

1984 he was reelected president.

1989 he returned home to California.

2004 he died on June 5, 2004. | Age 93

"The Wall Came Tumbling Down"

The world kept changing after Reagan left the White House. More and more voices in Communist countries were calling for freedom. In 1989, officials in East Berlin made an announcement. People from the eastern half of the city would be allowed to go to the west.

At once, thousands rushed to the Berlin Wall. They poured through the gates to the other side. After twenty-eight years, friends and family were together again.

Then people went to the wall with picks and hammers. Piece by piece, they began to tear down the wall. Bulldozers finished the job. In the end, there was little left.

Parts of the wall were sent to museums all over the world. One section was presented to Ronald Reagan. It was given to honor the U.S. president who once stood at the wall and spoke of freedom.

This section of the Berlin Wall stands outside the Ronald Reagan Presidential Library in California.

FURTHER READING

Sis, Peter. *The Wall: Growing Up Behind the Iron Curtain.* **New York: Farrar, Straus and Giroux, 2007.** Read about what it was like to grow up on the other side of the Berlin Wall.

Taylor, David. *The Cold War.* **Chicago: Heinemann Library, 2001.** This book explains the years when the United States and the Soviet Union did not trust each other.

Waxman, Laura Hamilton. *Jimmy Carter.* **Minneapolis: Lerner Publications Company, 2006.** This biography tells about the life of the thirty-ninth U.S. president.

Welch, Catherine A. *George H. W. Bush.* **Minneapolis: Lerner Publications Company, 2008.** Learn more about the man who served as Ronald Reagan's vice president and the forty-first president of the United States.

WEBSITES

American Experience: Reagan
http://www.pbs.org/wgbh/amex/reagan/
Learn more about Reagan and the important people and events in his life and career.

Berlin Wall Online
http://www.dailysoft.com/berlinwall/
Read about the history of the Berlin Wall, and see where to find pieces of the wall today.

Ronald Reagan Presidential Library
http://www.reagan.utexas.edu/
Find speeches, photographs, timelines, and other information about Ronald Reagan's life and career.

SELECT BIBLIOGRAPHY

Burkhardt, Heiko. "Berlin Wall History." *Berlin Wall Online.* 2008. http://www.dailysoft.com/berlinwall/ (March 20, 2008).

D'Souza, Dinesh. *Ronald Reagan: How an Ordinary Man Became an Extraordinary Leader.* New York: Free Press, 1997.

Kaiser, Robert G. "Gorbachev: We All Lost Cold War." *Washington Post,* June 11, 2004.

Morris, Edmund. *Dutch: A Memoir of Ronald Reagan.* New York: Random House, 1999.

Ratnesar, Romesh. "20 Years after 'Tear Down This Wall.'" *Time,* June 11, 2007. http://www.time.com/time/world/article/0,8599,1631828,00.html (March 20, 2008).

Reagan, Ronald. *An American Life.* New York: Simon & Schuster, 1990.

Reagan, Ronald. *The Reagan Diaries.* Edited by Douglas Brinkley. New York: HarperCollins, 2007.

Reagan, Ronald. *Reagan, in His Own Hand: The Writings of Ronald Reagan That Reveal His Revolutionary Vision for America.* New York: Free Press, 2001.

Reeves, Richard. *President Reagan: The Triumph of Imagination.* New York: Simon & Schuster, 2005.

Ronald Reagan Presidential Library and Museum. "The Public Papers of President Ronald W. Reagan." *Ronald Reagan Presidential Foundation and Library.* http://www.reagan.utexas.edu/archives/speeches/publicpapers.html (March 20, 2008).

INDEX

Acknowledgments

The images in this book are used with the permission of: Courtesy Ronald Reagan Library, pp. 4, 7, 9, 10, 11, 16, 20, 21, 22, 23, 24, 27, 28, 29, 31, 32, 33, 37, 38, 39, 40, 41, 42, 45; AP Photo, p. 14; KNUTE ROCKNE-ALL AMERICAN (1940) © Turner Entertainment Co. A Warner Bros. Entertainment Company. All Rights Reserved. Image courtesy Ronald Reagan Library, p. 15; © Bettmann/CORBIS, p. 25. Front cover: The White House. Back cover: © Todd Strand/Independent Picture Service. **For quoted material:** pp. 12, 13, 25, 30 (both), 33, 45, Ronald Reagan, *An American Life* (New York: Simon & Schuster, 1990); p. 17, Edmund Morris, *Dutch: A Memoir of Ronald Reagan* (New York: Random House, 1999); p. 36, Ronald Reagan, "Address to Nation on Explosion of Space Shuttle Challenger" (speech, White House, Washington, DC, January 28, 1986, available online at http://www.reagan .utexas.edu/archives/speeches/1986/12886b.htm); p. 37, Ronald Reagan, "Remarks on East-West Relations at the Brandenburg Gate in West Berlin" (speech, West Berlin, Germany, June 12, 1987, available online at http://www.reagan.utexas. edu/archives/speeches/1987/061287d.htm); p. 39, Ronald Reagan, "Address to the Nation on the Iran Arms and Contra Aid Controversy" (speech, White House, Washington, DC, March 4, 1987, available online at http://www.reagan.utexas.edu/ archives/speeches/1987/030487h.htm); p. 41, Richard Reeves, *President Reagan: The Triumph of Imagination* (New York: Simon & Schuster, 2005); p. 42, Ronald Reagan, "Farewell Address to the Nation" (speech, White House, Washington DC, January 11, 1989, available online at http://www.reagan.utexas.edu/archives/ speeches/1989/011189i.htm); p. 43, Robert G. Kaiser, "Gorbachev: We All Lost Cold War," *Washington Post*, June 11, 2004.